HERE COMES A
STORM

by Melissa Burke

Editorial Offices: Glenview, Illinois • Parsippany, New Jersey • New York, New York
Sales Offices: Needham, Massachusetts • Duluth, Georgia • Glenview, Illinois
Coppell, Texas • Ontario, California • Mesa, Arizona

What does a meteorologist do?

Have you ever had to change plans because of the weather? Maybe you've wished you could change the weather instead of your plans! Of course, we can't change the weather just because we don't like it, but there is something people can do to help with making plans. Some people work to **predict** the weather.

Predicting, or forecasting, weather is a science. It's a part of the study of weather called meteorology. The scientists who study weather are called **meteorologists.**

Why do we need to predict the weather?

Maybe you've seen a meteorologist on TV. TV meteorologists tell people about weather **conditions,** and make **forecasts** about the weather. Many people get their weather news from TV meteorologists.

People want to know what the weather will be like today, tomorrow, and next week. They want to know how to dress for outdoor activities. They need to know there will be good weather to travel.

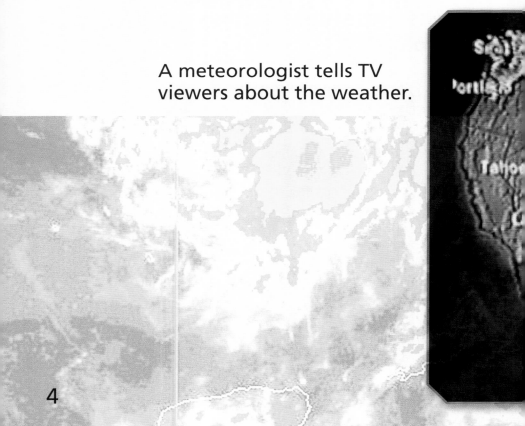

A meteorologist tells TV viewers about the weather.

People also need to know about weather so they can do their jobs. Farmers need to plan the best times to plant their crops. They need to know if they will ripen earlier or later than usual. Builders need to know the best time to start construction. Truck drivers and airplane pilots must know if it is safe to drive or fly. Many other jobs depend on weather too.

You can make a weather forecast yourself; just look out your window. Do you see any clouds? Step outside. Does it feel wet or dry? If there are no clouds and it feels dry, you could predict that it is not likely to rain.

This is a simple weather prediction based on a little bit of information. The kinds of predictions meteorologists make call for much more information.

Meteorologists can tell exactly how hot or how cold it is. They tell if it might rain or snow. They tell how fast the winds are blowing and what kinds of clouds there are. TV forecasters use a weather map or they may also use satellite and radar pictures.

Weather predictions help you decide if you need to dress for rain.

Gathering Information

Meteorologists work at weather stations. They are always busy gathering weather information. They **record** details about clouds, air temperature, air pressure, humidity, and wind. Special tools are used to collect this information.

To make forecasts, meteorologists gather information from around the world. Weather in one part of the world can affect weather in other places. Meteorologists work together with scientists from many places.

TIROS N is a spacecraft that helps forecast weather.

It is important that all scientists measure weather information the same way, using the same tools. Meteorologists around the world also use the same units of measurement. This way they can share the information they get. Let's look at some of the tools meteorologists use.

Meteorologists use thermometers to measure temperature. Temperature is how hot or how cold the air is. Temperature can be measured in Fahrenheit or in Celsius.

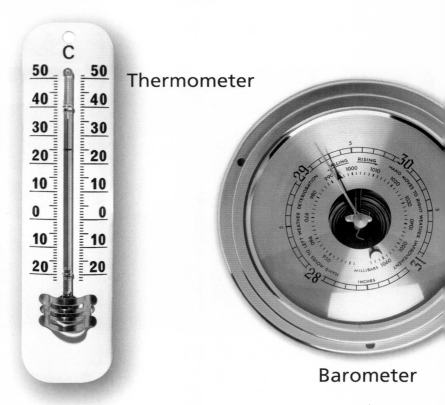

Thermometer

Barometer

Barometers are used to measure air pressure. Air pressure is measured in units called atmospheres.

Anemometers are used to measure the speed of the wind. Wind speed can be measured in miles or kilometers per hour.

Rain gauges are used to measure how much water falls to Earth. Rainfall is measured in inches or centimeters.

Anemometer

Rain gauge

Some tools are used to gather information above Earth. People fly special planes through clouds. The meteorologists in the planes report about conditions in the sky. Some planes even fly through **terrifying** storms to learn more about them. Scientists also send up weather balloons to get details at different heights. The scientist to the right is preparing to send a special weather balloon up into a storm.

Satellites fly around Earth in space. These machines can measure temperature and moisture. They also take pictures of clouds and storms. Scientists keep track of how these pictures change so that they can see how the clouds and storms are moving, or where they are going.

This weather balloon is called a Jimsphere. It provides information about the wind.

Scientists are at work creating more advanced satellites all the time.

Meteorologists also use weather radar. Radar is a tool that sends out radio waves from an antenna. The radio waves travel through the air. The waves bounce into objects, such as raindrops or hailstones. When this happens, some of the waves bounce back to the antenna.

The radar changes those radio waves into a picture. The picture shows where the rain or hail is happening. Radar can also tell about how winds are blowing.

Doppler weather radar

Making Forecasts

All this weather information is sent to major weather centers. Organizing all this information is quite difficult. Meteorologists use computers to help them put it all together.

Meteorologists spend a lot of time tracking storms. The storms may be very far away from their area. Meteorologists need to think about how the storms might move and change. They also think about new storms that may develop.

Mir space station over a hurricane

They use what they know about clouds, air temperature, moisture, air pressure, and wind. They try to find weather **patterns.** They review what has happened in the past and then they predict what will most likely happen again. Computers help meteorologists make these forecasts, then the meteorologists can tell people like you. They can give hurricane or tornado warnings when they see pictures like the one below.

Hurricane Nora

Even meteorologists don't always get the forecasts right. That's because the weather is always changing. Small differences in weather can cause sudden changes that the forecaster doesn't expect. Forecasters try to use patterns to tell what will happen next. But things don't always happen in a pattern.

Meteorologists make forecasts of hurricanes.

Becoming a Meteorologist

To become a meteorologist, you must go to college and learn a lot of math and science. You also need to learn how to use computers.

If you think you would like to become a meteorologist someday, there are things you can do right now. Watch weather forecasts. Read all that you can about weather. Ask your parents or a teacher to help you write to a TV meteorologist. Ask him or her questions.

Try coming up with your own ideas about weather and writing them in a journal. Make observations. Go back and check if you were right. If you want to give weather tracking a try, do the activity on the following pages.

Practice measuring and recording different kinds of weather.

Now Try This

Be a Weather Watcher

Meteorologists are weather watchers. You can be a weather watcher too! And what about watching meteorologists? See what you can learn by comparing some forecasts to what really happens.

S		Partly Cloudy	46°/38°
M		Rain	49°/45°
T		Showers	51°/36°
W		Partly Cloudy	46°/26°
T		Sunny	46°/38°
F		Partly Cloudy	46°/38°
S		Sunny	46°/38°

1. First, make a forecast chart like the one shown. Leave the all the columns blank except for the first column—the days of the week.

2. Watch or read a seven-day forecast from TV, the Internet, or a newspaper. Write down the forecast for each day.

3. Write down what the weather was really like each day.

4. Compare the forecasts to the actual weather. Did they match? Why do you think this is so?

19

Glossary

conditions *n.* the way that somethings are.

forecasts *n.* predictions about what is coming.

meteorologists *n.* people who study weather.

patterns *n.* things that repeat.

predict *v.* to tell what will happen next.

record *v.* to keep track of.

terrifying *adj.* very scary.